THE POEMS
OF
ALICE MEYNELL

COMPLETE EDITION

Alice Meynell
From a drawing by John S. Sargent, R.A.

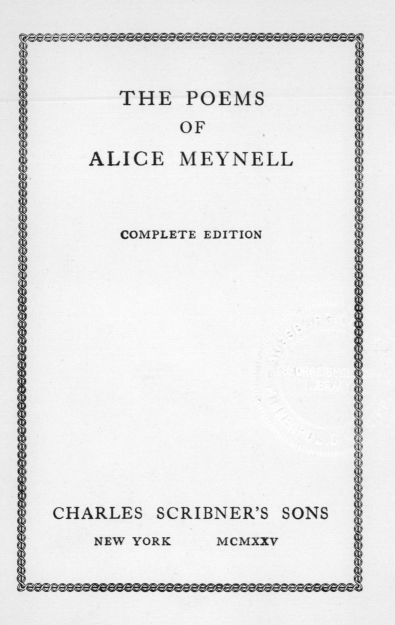

THE POEMS
OF
ALICE MEYNELL

COMPLETE EDITION

CHARLES SCRIBNER'S SONS

NEW YORK　　MCMXXV

To
W. M.

BIBLIOGRAPHICAL NOTE

This volume contains the whole of Mrs. Meynell's poetry: her early volume of "Preludes"; her "Poems," issued in 1893, of which nine impressions were printed before 1913, when it was incorporated in the Collected Edition; "Later Poems," issued in 1901, also incorporated in the edition of 1913; "Poems: Collected Edition," issued in 1913, of which the eighth impression was printed in 1919, and a ninth with additions in 1921; "A Father of Women, and other Poems," issued in 1918, and included in the Collected Edition in 1919; and finally "Last Poems," issued in February, 1923.

THE CONTENTS

EARLY POEMS

vii

THE CONTENTS

THE CONTENTS

ix

THE CONTENTS

LAST POEMS

THE CONTENTS

Early Poems

IN EARLY SPRING

O SPRING, I know thee! Seek for sweet surprise
    In the young children's eyes.
But I have learnt the years, and know the yet
    Leaf-folded violet.
Mine ear, awake to silence, can foretell
    The cuckoo's fitful bell.
I wander in a grey time that encloses
    June and the wild hedge-roses.
A year's procession of the flowers doth pass
    My feet, along the grass.
And all you wild birds silent yet, I know
    The notes that stir you so,
Your songs yet half devised in the dim dear
    Beginnings of the year.
In these young days you meditate your part;
    I have it all by heart.

I know the secrets of the seeds of flowers
    Hidden and warm with showers,
And how, in kindling Spring, the cuckoo shall
    Alter his interval.
But not a flower or song I ponder is
    My own, but memory's.
I shall be silent in those days desired
    Before a world inspired.
O all brown birds, compose your old song-phrases,
    Earth, thy familiar daisies!

A poet mused upon the dusky height,
    Between two stars towards night,
His purpose in his heart. I watched, a space,
    The meaning of his face:
There was the secret, fled from earth and skies,
    Hid in his grey young eyes.

3

IN EARLY SPRING

My heart and all the Summer wait his choice,
    And wonder for his voice.
Who shall foretell his songs, and who aspire
    But to divine his lyre?
Sweet earth, we know thy dimmest mysteries,
    But he is lord of his.

TO THE BELOVED

OH, not more subtly silence strays
    Amongst the winds, between the voices,
Mingling alike with pensive lays,
    And with the music that rejoices,
Than thou art present in my days.

My silence, life returns to thee
    In all the pauses of her breath.
Hush back to rest the melody
    That out of thee awakeneth;
And thou, wake ever, wake for me!

Thou art like silence all unvexed,
    Though wild words part my soul from thee.
Thou art like silence unperplexed,
    A secret and a mystery
Between one footfall and the next.

Most dear pause in a mellow lay!
    Thou art inwoven with every air.
With thee the wildest tempests play,
    And snatches of thee everywhere
Make little heavens throughout a day.

Darkness and solitude shine, for me.
    For life's fair outward part are rife
The silver noises; let them be.
    It is the very soul of life
Listens for thee, listens for thee.

TO THE BELOVED

O pause between the sobs of cares;
   O thought within all thought that is;
Trance between laughters unawares:
   Thou art the shape of melodies,
And thou the ecstasy of prayers!

AN UNMARKED FESTIVAL

THERE'S a feast undated, yet
   Both our true lives hold it fast,—
Even the day when first we met.
   What a great day came and passed,
   —Unknown then, but known at last.

And we met : You knew not me,
   Mistress of your joys and fears ;
Held my hand that held the key
   Of the treasure of your years,
   Of the fountain of your tears.

For you knew not it was I,
   And I knew not it was you.
We have learnt, as days went by.
   But a flower struck root and grew
   Underground, and no one knew.

Day of days ! Unmarked it rose,
   In whose hours we were to meet ;
And forgotten passed.   Who knows,
   Was earth cold or sunny, Sweet,
   At the coming of your feet?

One mere day, we thought ; the measure
   Of such days the year fulfils.
Now, how dearly would we treasure
   Something from its fields, its rills,
   And its memorable hills.

IN AUTUMN

THE leaves are many under my feet,
 And drift one way.
Their scent of death is weary and sweet.
 A flight of them is in the grey
Where sky and forest meet.

The low winds moan for dead sweet years;
 The birds sing all for pain,
Of a common thing, to weary ears,—
 Only a summer's fate of rain,
And a woman's fate of tears.

I walk to love and life alone
 Over these mournful places,
Across the summer overthrown,
 The dead joys of these silent faces,
To claim my own.

I know his heart has beat to bright
 Sweet loves gone by;
I know the leaves that die to-night
 Once budded to the sky;
And I shall die from his delight.

O leaves, so quietly ending now,
 You heard the cuckoos sing.
And I will grow upon my bough
 If only for a Spring,
And fall when the rain is on my brow.

8

IN AUTUMN

O tell me, tell me ere you die,
  Is it worth the pain?
You bloomed so fair, you waved so high;
  Now that the sad days wane,
Are you repenting where you lie?

I lie amongst you, and I kiss
  Your fragrance mouldering.
O dead delights, is it such bliss,
  That tuneful Spring?
Is love so sweet, that comes to this?

Kiss me again as I kiss you;
  Kiss me again,
For all your tuneful nights of dew,
  In this your time of rain,
For all your kisses when Spring was new.

You will not, broken hearts; let be.
  I pass across your death
To a golden summer you shall not see,
  And in your dying breath
There is no benison for me.

There is an autumn yet to wane,
  There are leaves yet to fall,
Which, when I kiss, may kiss again,
  And, pitied, pity me all for all,
And love me in mist and rain.

PARTED

FAREWELL to one now silenced quite,
  Sent out of hearing, out of sight,—
My friend of friends, whom I shall miss.
He is not banished, though, for this,—
Nor he, nor sadness, nor delight.

Though I shall talk with him no more,
A low voice sounds upon the shore.
  He must not watch my resting-place,
  But who shall drive a mournful face
From the sad winds about my door?

I shall not hear his voice complain,
But who shall stop the patient rain?
  His tears must not disturb my heart,
  But who shall change the years, and part
The world from every thought of pain?

Although my life is left so dim,
The morning crowns the mountain-rim;
  Joy is not gone from summer skies,
  Nor innocence from children's eyes,
And all these things are part of him.

He is not banished, for the showers
Yet wake this green warm earth of ours.
  How can the summer but be sweet?
  I shall not have him at my feet,
And yet my feet are on the flowers.

"SŒUR MONIQUE"

A Rondeau by Couperin

QUIET form of silent nun,
    What has given you to my inward eyes?
What has marked you, unknown one,
In the throngs of centuries
That mine ears do listen through?
This old master's melody
That expresses you ;
This admired simplicity,
Tender, with a serious wit ;
And two words, the name of it,
    "Sœur Monique."

And if sad the music is,
It is sad with mysteries
Of a small immortal thing
That the passing ages sing,—
Simple music making mirth
Of the dying and the birth
Of the people of the earth.

No, not sad ; we are beguiled,
Sad with living as we are ;
Ours the sorrow, outpouring
Sad self on a selfless thing,
As our eyes and hearts are mild
With our sympathy for Spring,
With a pity sweet and wild
For the innocent and far,
With our sadness in a star,
Or our sadness in a child.

"SŒUR MONIQUE"

But two words, and this sweet air.
    Sœur Monique,
Had he more, who set you there?
Was his music-dream of you
Of some perfect nun he knew,
Or of some ideal, as true?

And I see you where you stand
With your life held in your hand
As a rosary of days.
And your thoughts in calm arrays,
And your innocent prayers are told
On your rosary of days.
And the young days and the old
With their quiet prayers did meet
When the chaplet was complete.

Did it vex you, the surmise
Of this wind of words, this storm of cries,
    Though you kept the silence so
    In the storms of long ago,
    And you keep it, like a star?
    —Of the evils triumphing,
Strong, for all your perfect conquering,
    Silenced conqueror that you are?

And I wonder at your peace, I wonder.
Would it trouble you to know,
Tender soul, the world and sin
By your calm feet trodden under
    Long ago,
Living now, mighty to win?
And your feet are vanished like the snow.

12

"SŒUR MONIQUE"

Vanished ; but the poet, he
In whose dream your face appears,
He who ranges unknown years
With your music in his heart,
Speaks to you familiarly
Where you keep apart,
And invents you as you were.
And your picture, O my nun !
Is a strangely easy one,
For the holy weed you wear,
For your hidden eyes and hidden hair,
And in picturing you I may
Scarcely go astray.

O the vague reality,
The mysterious certainty !
O strange truth of these my guesses
In the wide thought-wildernesses !
—Truth of one divined of many flowers ;
Of one raindrop in the showers
Of the long ago swift rain;
Of one tear of many tears
In some world-renownèd pain ;
Of one daisy 'mid the centuries of sun ;
Of a little living nun
In the garden of the years.

Yes, I am not far astray ;
But I guess you as might one
Pausing when young March is grey,
In a violet-peopled day ;
All his thoughts go out to places that he knew,
To his child-home in the sun,
To the fields of his regret,
To one place i' the innocent March air,

"SŒUR MONIQUE"

By one olive, and invent
The familiar form and scent
Safely; a white violet
Certainly is there.

Sœur Monique, remember me.
'Tis not in the past alone
I am picturing you to be;
But my little friend, my own,
In my moment, pray for me.
For another dream is mine,
And another dream is true,
  Sweeter even,
Of the little ones that shine
Lost within the light divine,—
Of some meekest flower, or you,
  In the fields of heaven.

REGRETS

A S, when the seaward ebbing tide doth pour
    Out by the low sand spaces,
The parting waves slip back to clasp the shore
    With lingering embraces,—

So in the tide of life that carries me
    From where thy true heart dwells,
Waves of my thoughts and memories turn to thee
    With lessening farewells ;

Waving of hands ; dreams, when the day forgets ;
    A care half lost in cares ;
The saddest of my verses ; dim regrets ;
    Thy name among my prayers.

I would the day might come, so waited for,
    So patiently besought,
When I, returning, should fill up once more
    Thy desolated thought ;

And fill thy loneliness that lies apart
    In still, persistent pain.
Shall I content thee, O thou broken heart,
    As the tide comes again,

And brims the little sea-shore lakes, and sets
    Seaweeds afloat, and fills
The silent pools, rivers and rivulets
    Among the inland hills?

THE VISITING SEA

AS the inhastening tide doth roll,
   Home from the deep, along the whole
Wide shining strand, and floods the caves,
—Your love comes filling with happy waves
The open sea-shore of my soul.

But inland from the seaward spaces,
None knows, not even you, the places
   Brimmed, at your coming, out of sight,
   —The little solitudes of delight
This tide constrains in dim embraces.

You see the happy shore, wave-rimmed,
But know not of the quiet dimmed
   Rivers your coming floods and fills,
   The little pools 'mid happier hills,
My silent rivulets, over-brimmed.

What! I have secrets from you? Yes.
But, visiting Sea, your love doth press
   And reach in further than you know,
   And fills all these; and, when you go,
There's loneliness in loneliness.

AFTER A PARTING

FAREWELL has long been said ; I have
        foregone thee ;
    I never name thee even.
But how shall I learn virtues and yet shun thee?
    For thou art so near Heaven
That Heavenward meditations pause upon thee.

Thou dost beset the path to every shrine ;
    My trembling thoughts discern
Thy goodness in the good for which I pine ;
    And, if I turn from but one sin, I turn
Unto a smile of thine.

How shall I thrust thee apart
    Since all my growth tends to thee night and day—
To thee faith, hope, and art?
    Swift are the currents setting all one way ;
They draw my life, my life, out of my heart.

BUILDERS OF RUINS

WE build with strength the deep tower wall
   That shall be shattered thus and thus.
And fair and great are court and hall,
   But *how* fair—this is not for us,
Who know the lack that lurks in all.

We know, we know how all too bright
   The hues are that our painting wears,
And how the marble gleams too white;—
   We speak in unknown tongues, the years
Interpret everything aright,

And crown with weeds our pride of towers,
   And warm our marble through with sun,
And break our pavements through with flowers,
   With an Amen when all is done,
Knowing these perfect things of ours.

O days, we ponder, left alone,
   Like children in their lonely hour,
And in our secrets keep your own,
   As seeds the colour of the flower.
To-day they are not all unknown,

The stars that 'twixt the rise and fall,
   Like relic-seers, shall one by one
Stand musing o'er our empty hall;
   And setting moons shall brood upon
The frescoes of our inward wall.

BUILDERS OF RUINS

And when some midsummer shall be,
    Hither will come some little one
(Dusty with bloom of flowers is he),
    Sit on a ruin i' the late long sun,
And think, one foot upon his knee.

And where they wrought, these lives of ours,
    So many-worded, many-souled,
A North-west wind will take the towers,
    And dark with colour, sunny and cold,
Will range alone among the flowers.

And here or there, at our desire,
    The little clamorous owl shall sit
Through her still time; and we aspire
    To make a law (and know not it)
Unto the life of a wild briar.

Our purpose is distinct and dear,
    Though from our open eyes 'tis hidden.
Thou, Time to come, shalt make it clear,
    Undoing our work; we are children chidden
With pity and smiles of many a year.

Who shall allot the praise, and guess
    What part is yours and what is ours?—
O years that certainly will bless
    Our flowers with fruits, our seeds with flowers,
With ruin all our perfectness.

Be patient, Time, of our delays,
    Too happy hopes, and wasted fears,
Our faithful ways, our wilful ways;
    Solace our labours, O our seers
The seasons, and our bards the days;

BUILDERS OF RUINS

And make our pause and silence brim
    With the shrill children's play, and sweets
Of those pathetic flowers and dim,
    Of those eternal flowers my Keats
Dying felt growing over him !

THOUGHTS IN SEPARATION

WE never meet; yet we meet day by day
    Upon those hills of life, dim and immense—
The good we love, and sleep, our innocence.
O hills of life, high hills! And, higher than they,

Our guardian spirits meet at prayer and play.
    Beyond pain, joy, and hope, and long suspense,
    Above the summits of our souls, far hence,
An angel meets an angel on the way.

Beyond all good I ever believed of thee,
    Or thou of me, these always love and live.
And though I fail of thy ideal of me,

My angel falls not short. They greet each other.
    Who knows, they may exchange the kiss we give,
Thou to thy crucifix, I to my mother.

THE GARDEN

MY heart shall be thy garden. Come, my own,
　　Into thy garden; thine be happy hours
　Among my fairest thoughts, my tallest flowers,
From root to crowning petal thine alone.

Thine is the place from where the seeds are sown
　Up to the sky enclosed, with all its showers.
　　But ah, the birds, the birds!　Who shall build bowers
To keep these thine?　O friend, the birds have flown.

For as these come and go, and quit our pine
　To follow the sweet season, or, new-comers,
　　Sing one song only from our alder-trees,

My heart has thoughts, which, though thine eyes hold
　　mine,
　Flit to the silent world and other summers,
　　With wings that dip beyond the silver seas.

YOUR OWN FAIR YOUTH

YOUR own fair youth, you care so little for it—
    Smiling towards Heaven, you would not stay the
    advances
Of time and change upon your happiest fancies.
I keep your golden hour, and will restore it.

If ever, in time to come, you would explore it—
    Your old self, whose thoughts went like last year's
    pansies,
    Look unto me; no mirror keeps its glances;
In my unfailing praises now I store it.

To guard all joys of yours from Time's estranging,
    I shall be then a treasury where your gay,
    Happy, and pensive past unaltered is.

I shall be then a garden charmed from changing,
    In which your June has never passed away.
    Walk there awhile among my memories.

THE YOUNG NEOPHYTE

WHO knows what days I answer for to-day?
  Giving the bud I give the flower.   I bow
This yet unfaded and a faded brow;
Bending these knees and feeble knees, I pray.

Thoughts yet unripe in me I bend one way,
  Give one repose to pain I know not now,
  One check to joy that comes, I guess not how.
I dedicate my fields when Spring is grey.

O rash! (I smile) to pledge my hidden wheat.
  I fold to-day at altars far apart
Hands trembling with what toils?   In their retreat

  I seal my love to-be, my folded art.
I light the tapers at my head and feet,
  And lay the crucifix on this silent heart.

SPRING ON THE ALBAN HILLS

O'ER the Campagna it is dim warm weather;
   The Spring comes with a full heart silently,
And many thoughts; a faint flash of the sea
Divides two mists; straight falls the falling feather.

With wild Spring meanings hill and plain together
   Grow pale, or just flush with a dust of flowers.
   Rome in the ages, dimmed with all her towers,
Floats in the midst, a little cloud at tether.

I fain would put my hands about thy face,
   Thou with thy thoughts, who art another Spring,
   And draw thee to me like a mournful child.

Thou lookest on me from another place;
   I touch not this day's secret, nor the thing
   That in the silence makes thy soft eyes wild.

25

IN FEBRUARY

RICH meanings of the prophet-Spring adorn,
　　Unseen, this colourless sky of folded showers,
　And folded winds ; no blossom in the bowers ;
A poet's face asleep in this grey morn.

Now in the midst of the old world forlorn
　　A mystic child is set in these still hours.
　I keep this time, even before the flowers,
Sacred to all the young and the unborn :

To all the miles and miles of unsprung wheat,
　　And to the Spring waiting beyond the portal,
　　And to the future of my own young art,

And, among all these things, to you, my sweet,
　　My friend, to your calm face and the immortal
　　Child tarrying all your life-time in your heart.

A SHATTERED LUTE

I TOUCHED the heart that loved me as a player
   Touches a lyre.   Content with my poor skill,
 No touch save mine knew my beloved (and still
I thought at times : Is there no sweet lost air

Old loves could wake in him, I cannot share?)
   O he alone, alone could so fulfil
   My thoughts in sound to the measure of my will.
He is gone, and silence takes me unaware.

The songs I knew not he resumes, set free
From my constraining love, alas for me !
   His part in our tune goes with him ; my part

Is locked in me for ever ; I stand as mute
   As one with vigorous music in his heart
Whose fingers stray upon a shattered lute.

RENOUNCEMENT

I MUST not think of thee ; and, tired yet strong,
   I shun the thought that lurks in all delight—
The thought of thee—and in the blue Heaven's height,
And in the sweetest passage of a song.

O just beyond the fairest thoughts that throng
   This breast, the thought of thee waits, hidden yet
      bright ;
   But it must never, never come in sight ;
I must stop short of thee the whole day long.

But when sleep comes to close each difficult day,
   When night gives pause to the long watch I keep,
   And all my bonds I needs must loose apart,

Must doff my will as raiment laid away,—
   With the first dream that comes with the first sleep
   I run, I run, I am gathered to thy heart.

TO A DAISY

SLIGHT as thou art, thou art enough to hide
   Like all created things, secrets from me,
And stand a barrier to eternity.
And I, how can I praise thee well and wide

From where I dwell—upon the hither side?
      Thou little veil for so great mystery,
      When shall I penetrate all things and thee,
And then look back?   For this I must abide,

Till thou shalt grow and fold and be unfurled
Literally between me and the world.
      Then I shall drink from in beneath a spring,

And from a poet's side shall read his book.
   O daisy mine, what will it be to look
      From God's side even of such a simple thing?

SAN LORENZO'S MOTHER

I HAD not seen my son's dear face
  (He chose the cloister by God's grace)
    Since it had come to full flower-time.
    I hardly guessed at its perfect prime,
That folded flower of his dear face.

Mine eyes were veiled by mists of tears
When on a day in many years
    One of his Order came. I thrilled,
    Facing, I thought, that face fulfilled.
I doubted, for my mists of tears.

His blessing be with me for ever !
My hope and doubt were hard to sever.
    —That altered face, those holy weeds.
    I filled his wallet and kissed his beads,
And lost his echoing feet for ever.

If to my son my alms were given
I know not, and I wait for Heaven.
    He did not plead for child of mine,
    But for another Child divine,
And unto Him it was surely given.

There is One alone who cannot change ;
Dreams are we, shadows, visions strange ;
    And all I give is given to One.
    I might mistake my dearest son,
But never the Son who cannot change.

THE LOVER URGES THE BETTER THRIFT

MY Fair, no beauty of thine will last
    Save in my love's eternity.
    Thy smiles, that light thee fitfully,
Are lost for ever—their moment past—
    Except the few thou givest to me.

Thy sweet words vanish day by day,
    As all breath of mortality;
    Thy laughter, done, must cease to be,
And all thy dear tones pass away,
    Except the few that sing to me.

Hide then within my heart, O hide
    All thou art loth should go from thee.
    Be kinder to thyself and me.
My cupful from this river's tide
    Shall never reach the long sad sea.

CRADLE-SONG AT TWILIGHT

THE child not yet is lulled to rest.
  Too young a nurse, the slender Night
So laxly holds him to her breast
  That throbs with flight.

He plays with her, and will not sleep.
  For other playfellows she sighs;
An unmaternal fondness keep
  Her alien eyes.

SONG OF THE NIGHT AT DAYBREAK

ALL my stars forsake me.
    And the dawn-winds shake me,
Where shall I betake me?

Whither shall I run
Till the set of sun,
Till the day be done?

To the mountain-mine,
To the boughs o' the pine,
To the blind man's eyne,

To a brow that is
Bowed upon the knees,
Sick with memories?

A LETTER FROM A GIRL TO HER OWN OLD AGE

LISTEN, and when thy hand this paper presses,
  O time-worn woman, think of her who blesses
What thy thin fingers touch, with her caresses.

O mother, for the weight of years that break thee!
O daughter, for slow time must yet awake thee,
And from the changes of my heart must make thee!

O fainting traveller, morn is grey in heaven.
Dost thou remember how the clouds were driven?
And are they calm about the fall of even?

Pause near the ending of thy long migration,
For this one sudden hour of desolation
Appeals to one hour of thy meditation.

Suffer, O silent one, that I remind thee
Of the great hills that stormed the sky behind thee,
Of the wild winds of power that have resigned thee.

Know that the mournful plain where thou must wander
Is but a grey and silent world, but ponder
The misty mountains of the morning yonder.

Listen:—the mountain winds with rain were fretting,
And sudden gleams the mountain-tops besetting.
I cannot let thee fade to death, forgetting.

34

A LETTER FROM A GIRL

What part of this wild heart of mine I know not
Will follow with thee where the great winds blow not,
And where the young flowers of the mountain grow not.

Yet let my letter with thy lost thoughts in it
Tell what the way was when thou didst begin it,
And win with thee the goal when thou shalt win it.

Oh, in some hour of thine thy thoughts shall guide thee.
Suddenly, though time, darkness, silence, hide thee,
This wind from thy lost country flits beside thee,—

Telling thee : all thy memories moved the maiden,
With thy regrets was morning over-shaden,
With sorrow, thou hast left, her life was laden.

But whither shall my thoughts turn to pursue thee?
Life changes, and the years and days renew thee.
Oh, Nature brings my straying heart unto thee.

Her winds will join us, with their constant kisses
Upon the evening as the morning tresses,
Her summers breathe the same unchanging blisses.

And we, so altered in our shifting phases,
Track one another 'mid the many mazes
By the eternal child-breath of the daisies.

I have not writ this letter of divining
To make a glory of thy silent pining,
A triumph of thy mute and strange declining.

35

A LETTER FROM A GIRL

Only one youth, and the bright life was shrouded.
Only one morning, and the day was clouded.
And one old age with all regrets is crowded.

O hush, O hush ! Thy tears my words are steeping.
O hush, hush, hush ! So full, the fount of weeping?
Poor eyes, so quickly moved, so near to sleeping?

Pardon the girl ; such strange desires beset her.
Poor woman, lay aside the mournful letter
That breaks thy heart ; the one who wrote, forget her :

The one who now thy faded features guesses,
With filial fingers thy grey hair caresses,
With morning tears thy mournful twilight blesses.

ADVENT MEDITATION

Rorate cœli desuper, et nubes pluant Justum
Aperiatur terra, et germinet Salvatorem.

NO sudden thing of glory and fear
Was the Lord's coming; but the dear
Slow Nature's days followed each other
To form the Saviour from his Mother
—One of the children of the year.

The earth, the rain, received the trust,
—The sun and dews, to frame the Just.
He drew His daily life from these,
According to His own decrees
Who makes man from the fertile dust.

Sweet summer and the winter wild,
These brought him forth, the Undefiled.
The happy Springs renewed again
His daily bread, the growing grain,
The food and raiment of the Child.

A POET'S FANCIES

I

THE LOVE OF NARCISSUS

LIKE him who met his own eyes in the river,
　　The poet trembles at his own long gaze
That meets him through the changing nights
　　and days
From out great Nature; all her waters quiver
With his fair image facing him for ever;
　　The music that he listens to betrays
　　His own heart to his ears; by trackless ways
His wild thoughts tend to him in long endeavour.

His dreams are far among the silent hills;
　　His vague voice calls him from the darkened plain
With winds at night; strange recognition thrills
　　His lonely heart with piercing love and pain;
He knows again his mirth in mountain rills,
　　His weary tears that touch him with the rain.

II

TO ANY POET

THOU who singest through the earth
　　All the earth's wild creatures fly thee;
Everywhere thou marrest mirth,—
　　　　Dumbly they defy thee;
　　There is something they deny thee.

A POET'S FANCIES

Pines thy fallen nature ever
For the unfallen Nature sweet.
But she shuns thy long endeavour,
    Though her flowers and wheat
Throng and press thy pausing feet.

Though thou tame a bird to love thee,
Press thy face to grass and flowers,
All these things reserve above thee,
    Secrets in the bowers,
Secrets in the sun and showers.

Sing thy sorrow, sing thy gladness,
In thy songs must wind and tree
Bear the fictions of thy sadness,
    Thy humanity.
For their truth is not for thee.

Wait, and many a secret nest,
Many a hoarded winter-store
Will be hidden on thy breast.
    Things thou longest for
Will not fear or shun thee more.

Thou shalt intimately lie
In the roots of flowers that thrust
Upwards from thee to the sky,
    With no more distrust
When they blossom from thy dust.

Silent labours of the rain
Shall be near thee, reconciled;
Little lives of leaves and grain,
    All things shy and wild,
Tell thee secrets, quiet child.

39

A POET'S FANCIES

Earth, set free from thy fair fancies
And the art thou shalt resign,
Will bring forth her rue and pansies
    Unto more divine
Thoughts than any thoughts of thine.

Nought will fear thee, humbled creature.
There will lie thy mortal burden
Pressed unto the heart of Nature,
    Songless in a garden,
With a long embrace of pardon.

Then the truth all creatures tell,
And His will Whom thou entreatest,
Shall absorb thee; there shall dwell
    Silence, the completest
Of thy poems, last and sweetest.

III

TO ONE POEM IN A SILENT TIME

WHO looked for thee, thou little song of mine?
    This winter of a silent poet's heart
Is suddenly sweet with thee. But what thou art,
Mid-winter flower, I would I could divine.

Art thou a last one, orphan of thy line?
    Did the dead summer's last warmth foster thee?
    Or is Spring folded up unguessed in me,
And stirring out of sight,—and thou the sign?

A POET'S FANCIES

Where shall I look—backwards or to the morrow
  For others of thy fragrance, secret child?
    Who knows if last things or if first things claim
      thee?

—Whether thou be the last smile of my sorrow,
  Or else a joy too sweet, a joy too wild.
    How, my December violet, shall I name thee?

IV

THE MOON TO THE SUN

The Poet sings to her Poet

AS the full moon shining there
  To the sun that lighteth her
Am I unto thee for ever,
O my secret glory-giver!
O my light, I am dark but fair,
    Black but fair.

Shine, Earth loves thee! And then shine
And be loved through thoughts of mine.
All thy secrets that I treasure
I translate them at my pleasure.
I am crowned with glory of thine,
    Thine, not thine.

I make pensive thy delight,
And thy strong gold silver-white.
Though all beauty of mine thou makest,
Yet to earth which thou forsakest
I have made thee fair all night,
    Day all night.

V

THE SPRING TO THE SUMMER

The Poet sings to her Poet

O POET of the time to be,
  My conqueror, I began for thee.
Enter into thy poet's pain,
And take the riches of the rain,
And make the perfect year for me.

Thou unto whom my lyre shall fall,
Whene'er thou comest, hear my call.
  O keep the promise of my lays,
  Take thou the parable of my days;
I trust thee with the aim of all.

And if thy thoughts unfold from me,
Know that I too have hints of thee,
  Dim hopes that come across my mind
  In the rare days of warmer wind,
And tones of summer in the sea.

And I have set thy paths, I guide
Thy blossoms on the wild hillside.
  And I, thy bygone poet, share
  The flowers that throng thy feet where'er
I led thy feet before I died.

VI

THE DAY TO THE NIGHT

The Poet sings to his Poet

FROM dawn to dusk, and from dusk to dawn,
  We two are sundered always, Sweet.
A few stars shake o'er the rocky lawn
  And the cold sea-shore when we meet.
  The twilight comes with thy shadowy feet.

We are not day and night, my Fair,
  But one. It is an hour of hours.
And thoughts that are not otherwhere
  Are thought here 'mid the blown sea-flowers,
  This meeting and this dusk of ours.

Delight has taken Pain to her heart,
  And there is dusk and stars for these.
O linger, linger! They would not part;
  And the wild wind comes from over-seas,
  With a new song to the olive trees.

And when we meet by the sounding pine
  Sleep draws near to his dreamless brother.
And when thy sweet eyes answer mine,
  Peace nestles close to her mournful mother,
  And Hope and Weariness kiss each other.

VII

A POET OF ONE MOOD

A POET of one mood in all my lays,
    Ranging all life to sing one only love,
    Like a west wind across the world I move,
Sweeping my harp of floods mine own wild ways.

The countries change, but not the west-wind days
    Which are my songs. My soft skies shine above,
    And on all seas the colours of a dove,
And on all fields a flash of silver greys.

I make the whole world answer to my art
    And sweet monotonous meanings. In your ears
I change not ever, bearing, for my part,
    One thought that is the treasure of my years
A small cloud full of rain upon my heart
    And in mine arms, clasped, like a child in tears.

VIII

A SONG OF DERIVATIONS

I COME from nothing; but from where
    Come the undying thoughts I bear?
    Down, through long links of death and birth,
    From the past poets of the earth,
My immortality is there.

44

A POET'S FANCIES

I am like the blossom of an hour,
But long, long vanished sun and shower
   Awoke my breath i' the young world's air;
   I track the past back everywhere
Through seed and flower and seed and flower.

Or I am like a stream that flows
Full of the cold springs that arose
   In morning lands, in distant hills;
   And down the plain my channel fills
With melting of forgotten snows.

Voices, I have not heard, possessed
My own fresh songs; my thoughts are blessed
   With relics of the far unknown.
   And mixed with memories not my own
The sweet streams throng into my breast.

Before this life began to be,
The happy songs that wake in me
   Woke long ago and far apart.
   Heavily on this little heart
Presses this immortality.

IX

SINGERS TO COME

NO new delights to our desire
   The singers of the past can yield.
I lift mine eyes to hill and field,
And see in them your yet dumb lyre,
   Poets unborn and unrevealed.

A POET'S FANCIES

Singers to come, what thoughts will start
  To song? What words of yours be sent
  Through man's soul, and with earth be blent?
These worlds of nature and the heart
  Await you like an instrument.

Who knows what musical flocks of words
  Upon these pine-tree tops will light,
  And crown these towers in circling flight,
And cross these seas like summer birds,
  And give a voice to the day and night?

Something of you already is ours;
  Some mystic part of you belongs
  To us whose dreams your future throngs,
Who look on hills, and trees, and flowers,
  Which will mean so much in your songs.

I wonder, like the maid who found,
  And knelt to lift, the lyre supreme
  Of Orpheus from the Thracian stream.
She dreams on its sealed past profound;
  On a deep future sealed I dream.

She bears it in her wanderings
  Within her arms, and has not pressed
  Her unskilled fingers, but her breast
Upon those silent sacred strings;
  I, too, clasp mystic strings at rest.

For I, i' the world of lands and seas,
  The sky of wind and rain and fire,
  And in man's world of long desire—
In all that is yet dumb in these—
  Have found a more mysterious lyre.

46

X

UNLINKED

IF I should quit thee, sacrifice, forswear,
  To what, my art, shall I give thee in keeping?
To the long winds of heaven? Shall these come sweeping
My songs forgone against my face and hair?

Or shall the mountain streams my lost joys bear,
  My past poetic in rain be weeping?
  No, I shall live a poet waking, sleeping,
And I shall die a poet unaware.

From me, my art, thou canst not pass away;
  And I, a singer though I cease to sing,
    Shall own thee without joy in thee or woe.

Through my indifferent words of every day,
  Scattered and all unlinked the rhymes shall ring,
    And make my poem; and I shall not know.

Later Poems

THE SHEPHERDESS

SHE walks—the lady of my delight—
  A shepherdess of sheep.
Her flocks are thoughts.   She keeps them white;
  She guards them from the steep;
She feeds them on the fragrant height,
  And folds them in for sleep.

She roams maternal hills and bright,
  Dark valleys safe and deep.
Into that tender breast at night
  The chastest stars may peep.
She walks—the lady of my delight—
  A shepherdess of sheep.

She holds her little thoughts in sight,
  Though gay they run and leap.
She is so circumspect and right;
  She has her soul to keep.
She walks—the lady of my delight—
  A shepherdess of sheep.

THE TWO POETS

WHOSE is the speech
That moves the voices of this lonely beech?
Out of the long west did this wild wind come—
O strong and silent! And the tree was dumb,
Ready and dumb, until
The dumb gale struck it on the darkened hill.

Two memories,
Two powers, two promises, two silences
Closed in this cry, closed in these thousand leaves
Articulate. This sudden hour retrieves
The purpose of the past,
Separate, apart—embraced, embraced at last.

"Whose is the word?
Is it I that spake? Is it thou? Is it I that heard?"
"Thine earth was solitary, yet I found thee!"
"Thy sky was pathless, but I caught, I bound thee,
Thou visitant divine."
"O thou my Voice, the word was thine." "Was thine."

THE LADY POVERTY

THE Lady Poverty was fair :
    But she has lost her looks of late,
With change of times and change of air.
Ah slattern ! she neglects her hair,
Her gown, her shoes ; she keeps no state
As once when her pure feet were bare.

Or—almost worse, if worse can be—
She scolds in parlours, dusts and trims,
Watches and counts.   O is this she
Whom Francis met, whose step was free,
Who with Obedience carolled hymns,
In Umbria walked with Chastity?

Where is her ladyhood? Not here,
Not among modern kinds of men ;
But in the stony fields, where clear
Through the thin trees the skies appear,
In delicate spare soil and fen,
And slender landscape and austere.

NOVEMBER BLUE

*The golden tint of the electric lights seems to give a comple-
mentary colour to the air in the early evening.*—ESSAY ON
LONDON.

O HEAVENLY colour, London town
   Has blurred it from her skies ;
And, hooded in an earthly brown,
   Unheaven'd the city lies.
No longer, standard-like, this hue
   Above the broad road flies ;
Nor does the narrow street the blue
   Wear, slender pennon-wise.

But when the gold and silver lamps
   Colour the London dew,
And, misted by the winter damps,
   The shops shine bright anew—
Blue comes to earth, it walks the street,
   It dyes the wide air through ;
A mimic sky about their feet,
   The throng go crowned with blue.

A DEAD HARVEST

IN KENSINGTON GARDENS

ALONG the graceless grass of town
 They rake the rows of red and brown,—
Dead leaves, unlike the rows of hay
Delicate, touched with gold and grey,
Raked long ago and far away.

A narrow silence in the park,
Between the lights a narrow dark,
One street rolls on the north; and one,
Muffled, upon the south doth run;
Amid the mist the work is done.

A futile crop !—for it the fire
Smoulders, and, for a stack, a pyre.
So go the town's lives on the breeze,
Even as the sheddings of the trees;
Bosom nor barn is filled with these.

THE WATERSHED

Lines written between Munich and Verona

BLACK mountains pricked with pointed pine
   A melancholy sky.
Out-distanced was the German vine,
   The sterile fields lay high.
From swarthy Alps I travelled forth
Aloft; it was the north, the north;
   Bound for the Noon was I.

I seemed to breast the streams that day;
   I met, opposed, withstood
The northward rivers on their way,
   My heart against the flood—
My heart that pressed to rise and reach,
And felt the love of altering speech,
   Of frontiers, in its blood.

But O the unfolding South! the burst
   Of summer! O to see
Of all the southward brooks the first!
   The travelling heart went free
With endless streams; that strife was stopped;
And down a thousand vales I dropped,
   I flowed to Italy.

THE JOYOUS WANDERER

Translated from M. Catulle Mendès

I GO by road, I go by street—
    Lira, la, la !
O white highways, ye know my feet !
A loaf I carry and, all told,
Three broad bits of lucky gold—
    Lira, la, la !
And O within my flowering heart,
(Sing, dear nightingale !) is my Sweet.

A poor man met me and begged for bread—
    Lira, la, la !
"Brother, take all the loaf," I said,
I shall but go with lighter cheer—
    Lira, la, la !
And O within my flowering heart
(Sing, sweet nightingale !) is my Dear.

A thief I met on the lonely way—
    Lira, la, la !
He took my gold ; I cried to him, "Stay !
And take my pocket and make an end."
    Lira, la, la !
And O within my flowering heart
(Sing, soft nightingale !) is my Friend.

Now on the plain I have met with death—
    Lira, la, la !
My bread is gone, my gold, my breath.
But O this heart is not afraid—
    Lira, la, la !
For O within this lonely heart
(Sing, sad nightingale !) is my Maid.

THE RAINY SUMMER

THERE'S much afoot in heaven and earth this year;
   The winds hunt up the sun, hunt up the moon,
Trouble the dubious dawn, hasten the drear
   Height of a threatening noon.

No breath of boughs, no breath of leaves, of fronds,
   May linger or grow warm; the trees are loud;
The forest, rooted, tosses in her bonds,
   And strains against the cloud.

No scents may pause within the garden-fold;
   The rifled flowers are cold as ocean-shells;
Bees, humming in the storm, carry their cold
   Wild honey to cold cells.

THE ROARING FROST

A FLOCK of winds came winging from the North,
Strong birds with fighting pinions driving forth
With a resounding call :—

Where will they close their wings and cease their cries—
Between what warming seas and conquering skies—
And fold, and fall?

WEST WIND IN WINTER

ANOTHER day awakes. And who—
    Changing the world—is this?
He comes at whiles, the winter through,
    West Wind! I would not miss
His sudden tryst: the long, the new
    Surprises of his kiss.

Vigilant, I make haste to close
    With him who comes my way,
I go to meet him as he goes;
    I know his note, his lay,
His colour and his morning-rose,
    And I confess his day.

My window waits; at dawn I hark
    His call; at morn I meet
His haste around the tossing park
    And down the softened street;
The gentler light is his: the dark,
    The grey—he turns it sweet.

So too, so too, do I confess
    My poet when he sings.
He rushes on my mortal guess
    With his immortal things.
I feel, I know, him. On I press—
    He finds me 'twixt his wings.

THE FOLD

BEHOLD,
  The time is now! Bring back, bring back
Thy flocks of fancies, wild of whim.
O lead them from the mountain-track
    Thy frolic thoughts untold,
O bring them in—the fields grow dim—
    And let me be the fold!

    Behold,
The time is now! Call in, O call
Thy pasturing kisses gone astray
For scattered sweets; gather them all
    To shelter from the cold.
Throng them together, close and gay,
    And let me be the fold!

"WHY WILT THOU CHIDE?"

WHY wilt thou chide,
     Who hast attained to be denied?
O learn, above
All price is my refusal, Love.
     My sacred Nay
Was never cheapened by the way.
Thy single sorrow crowns thee lord
Of an unpurchasable word.

     O strong, O pure !
As Yea makes happier loves secure,
     I vow thee this
Unique rejection of a kiss.
     I guard for thee
This jealous sad monopoly.
I seal this honour thine ; none dare
Hope for a part in thy despair.

VENERATION OF IMAGES

THOU man, first-comer, whose wide arms entreat,
   Gather, clasp, welcome, bind,
Lack, or remember; whose warm pulses beat
   With love of thine own kind :—

Unlifted for a blessing on yon sea,
   Unshrined on this highway,
O flesh, O grief, thou too shalt have our knee,
   Thou rood of every day !

"I AM THE WAY"

THOU art the Way.
   Hadst Thou been nothing but the goal,
      I cannot say
If Thou hadst ever met my soul.

      I cannot see—
I, child of process—if there lies
      An end for me,
Full of repose, full of replies.

      I'll not reproach
The road that winds, my feet that err,
      Access, Approach
Art Thou, Time, Way, and Wayfarer.

VIA, ET VERITAS, ET VITA

"YOU never attained to Him?"   "If to attain
     Be to abide, then that may be."
"Endless the way, followed with how much
          pain!"
     "The way was He."

PARENTAGE

*"When Augustus Cæsar legislated against the unmarried
citizens of Rome, he declared them to be, in some sort, slayers
of the people."*

AH! no, not these!
These, who were childless, are not they who gave
So many dead unto the journeying wave,
The helpless nurselings of the cradling seas;
Not they who doomed by infallible decrees
Unnumbered man to the innumerable grave.

But those who slay
Are fathers. Theirs are armies. Death is theirs—
The death of innocences and despairs;
The dying of the golden and the grey.
The sentence, when these speak it, has no Nay.
And she who slays is she who bears, who bears.

THE MODERN MOTHER

OH, what a kiss
    With filial passion overcharged is this !
      To this misgiving breast
This child runs, as a child ne'er ran to rest
Upon the light heart and the unoppressed.

      Unhoped, unsought !
A little tenderness, this mother thought
      The utmost of her meed.
She looked for gratitude ; content indeed
With thus much that her nine years' love had bought.

      Nay, even with less.
This mother, giver of life, death, peace, distress,
      Desired ah ! not so much
Thanks as forgiveness ; and the passing touch
Expected, and the slight, the brief caress.

      O filial light
Strong in these childish eyes, these new, these bright
      Intelligible stars !   Their rays
Are near the constant earth, guides in the maze,
Natural, true, keen in this dusk of days.

UNTO US A SON IS GIVEN

GIVEN, not lent,
   And not withdrawn—once sent,
This Infant of mankind, this One,
Is still the little welcome Son.

New every year,
New born and newly dear,
He comes with tidings and a song,
The ages long, the ages long;

Even as the cold
Keen winter grows not old,
As childhood is so fresh, foreseen,
And spring in the familiar green—

Sudden as sweet
Come the expected feet.
All joy is young, and new all art,
And He, too, Whom we have by heart.

VENI CREATOR

SO humble things Thou hast borne for us, O God,
Left'st Thou a path of lowliness untrod?
Yes, one, till now; another Olive-Garden.
For we endure the tender pain of pardon,—
One with another we forbear. Give heed,
Look at the mournful world Thou hast decreed.
The time has come. At last we hapless men
Know all our haplessness all through. Come, then,
Endure undreamed humility: Lord of Heaven,
Come to our ignorant hearts and be forgiven.

TWO BOYHOODS

LUMINOUS passions reign
    High in the soul of man; and they are twain.
Of these he hath made the poetry of earth—
Hath made his nobler tears, his magic mirth.

        Fair Love is one of these,
The visiting vision of seven centuries;
And one is love of Nature—love to tears—
The modern passion of this hundred years.

        O never to such height,
O never to such spiritual light—
The light of lonely visions, and the gleam
Of secret splendid sombre suns in dream—

        O never to such long
Glory in life, supremacy in song,
Had either of these loves attained in joy,
But for the ministration of a boy.

        Dante was one who bare
Love in his deep heart, apprehended there
When he was yet a child; and from that day
The radiant love has never passed away.

        And one was Wordsworth; he
Conceived the love of Nature childishly
As no adult heart might; old poets sing
That exaltation by remembering.

TWO BOYHOODS

For no divine
Intelligence, or art, or fire, or wine,
Is high-delirious as that rising lark—
The child's soul and its daybreak in the dark.

And Letters keep these two
Heavenly treasures safe the ages through,
Safe from ignoble benison or ban—
These two high childhoods in the heart of man.

TO SYLVIA

TWO YEARS OLD

LONG life to thee, long virtue, long delight,
   A flowering early and late!
Long beauty, grave to thought and gay to sight,
   A distant date!

Yet, as so many poets love to sing
   (When young the child will die),
"No autumn will destroy this lovely spring,"
   So, Sylvia, I.

I'll write thee dapper verse and touching rhyme;
   "Our eyes shall not behold—"
The commonplace shall serve for thee this time:
   "Never grow old."

For there's another way to stop thy clock
   Within my cherishing heart,
To carry thee unalterable, and lock
   Thy youth apart:

Thy flower, for me, shall evermore be hid
   In this close bud of thine,
Not, Sylvia, by thy death—O God forbid!
   Merely by mine.

SAINT CATHERINE OF SIENA

Written for Strephon, who said that a woman must lean, or she should not have his chivalry.

THE light young man who was to die,
    Stopped in his frolic by the State,
Aghast, beheld the world go by;
    But Catherine crossed his dungeon gate.

She found his lyric courage dumb,
    His stripling beauties strewn in wrecks,
His modish bravery overcome;
    Small profit had he of his sex.

On any old wife's level he,
    For once—for all. But he alone—
Man—must not fear the mystery,
    The pang, the passage, the unknown:

Death. He did fear it, in his cell,
    Darkling amid the Tuscan sun;
And, weeping, at her feet he fell,
    The sacred, young, provincial nun.

She prayed, she preached him innocent;
    She gave him to the Sacrificed;
On her courageous breast he leant,
    The breast where beat the heart of Christ.

He left it for the block, with cries
    Of victory on his severed breath.
That crimson head she clasped, her eyes
    Blind with the splendour of his death.

73

SAINT CATHERINE OF SIENA

And will the man of modern years
   —Stern on the Vote—withhold from thee,
Thou prop, thou cross, erect, in tears,
   Catherine, the service of his knee?

CHIMES

BRIEF, on a flying night,
  From the shaken tower,
A flock of bells take flight.
  And go with the hour.

Like birds from the cote to the gales,
  Abrupt—O hark !
A fleet of bells set sails,
  And go to the dark.

Sudden the cold airs swing.
  Alone, aloud,
A verse of bells takes wing
  And flies with the cloud.

A POET'S WIFE

I SAW a tract of ocean locked inland,
  Within a field's embrace—
The very sea! Afar it fled the strand,
  And gave the seasons chase,
And met the night alone, the tempest spanned,
  Saw sunrise face to face.

O Poet, more than ocean, lonelier!
  In inaccessible rest
And storm remote, thou sea of thoughts, dost stir
  Scattered through east to west,—
  Now, while thou closest with the kiss of her
  Who locks thee to her breast.

MESSINA, 1908

LORD, Thou hast crushed Thy tender ones, o'er-
        thrown
    Thy strong, Thy fair; Thy man thou hast un-
        manned,
Thy elaborate works unwrought, Thy deeds undone,
    Thy lovely sentient human plan unplanned;
Destroyer, we have cowered beneath Thine own
    Immediate, unintelligible hand.

Lord, thou hast hastened to retrieve, to heal,
    To feed, to bind, to clothe, to quench the brand,
To prop the ruin, to bless, and to anneal;
    Hast sped Thy ships by sea, Thy trains by land,
Shed pity and tears :—our shattered fingers feel
    Thy mediate and intelligible hand.

THE UNKNOWN GOD

ONE of the crowd went up,
   And knelt before the Paten and the Cup,
Received the Lord, returned in peace, and prayed
Close to my side.   Then in my heart I said :

"O Christ, in this man's life—
This stranger who is Thine—in all his strife,
All his felicity, his good and ill,
In the assaulted stronghold of his will,

"I do confess Thee here,
Alive within this life ; I know Thee near
Within this lonely conscience, closed away
Within this brother's solitary day.

"Christ in his unknown heart,
His intellect unknown—this love, this art,
This battle and this peace, this destiny
That I shall never know, look upon me !

"Christ in his numbered breath,
Christ in his beating heart and in his death,
Christ in his mystery !   From that secret place
And from that separate dwelling, give me grace !"

A GENERAL COMMUNION

I SAW the throng, so deeply separate,
    Fed at one only board—
The devout people, moved, intent, elate,
    And the devoted Lord.

O struck apart! not side from human side,
    But soul from human soul,
As each asunder absorbed the multiplied,
    The ever unparted, whole.

I saw this people as a field of flowers,
    Each grown at such a price
The sum of unimaginable powers
    Did no more than suffice.

A thousand single central daisies they,
    A thousand of the one;
For each, the entire monopoly of day;
    For each, the whole of the devoted sun.

THE FUGITIVE

"Nous avons chassé ce Jésus-Christ."—FRENCH PUBLICIST

YES, from the ingrate heart, the street
　　Of garrulous tongue, the warm retreat
Within the village and the town;
　　Not from the lands where ripen brown
A thousand thousand hills of wheat;

Not from the long Burgundian line,
The Southward, sunward range of vine.
　　Hunted, He never will escape
　　The flesh, the blood, the sheaf, the grape,
That feed His man—the bread, the wine.

IN PORTUGAL, 1912

AND will they cast the altars down,
   Scatter the chalice, crush the bread?
In field, in village, and in town
   He hides an unregarded head;

Waits in the corn-lands far and near,
   Bright in His sun, dark in His frost,
Sweet in the vine, ripe in the ear—
   Lonely unconsecrated Host.

In ambush at the merry board
   The Victim lurks unsacrificed;
The mill conceals the harvest's Lord,
   The wine-press holds the unbidden Christ.

THE CRUCIFIXION

"A Paltry Sacrifice."—PREFACE TO A PLAY

OH, man's capacity
    For spiritual sorrow, corporal pain!
Who has explored the deepmost of that sea,
With heavy links of a far-fathoming chain?

        That melancholy lead,
Let down in guilty and in innocent hold,
Yea into childish hands deliverèd,
Leaves the sequestered floor unreached, untold.

        One only has explored
The deepmost; but He did not die of it.
Not yet, not yet He died.   Man's human Lord
Touched the extreme; it is not infinite.

        But over the abyss
Of God's capacity for woe He stayed
One hesitating hour; what gulf was this?
Forsaken He went down, and was afraid.

THE NEWER VAINGLORY

TWO men went up to pray; and one gave thanks,
    Not with himself—aloud,
With proclamation, calling on the ranks
    Of an attentive crowd.

"Thank God, I clap not my own humble breast,
    But other ruffians' backs,
Imputing crime—such is my tolerant haste—
    To any man that lacks.

"For I am tolerant, generous, keep no rules,
    And the age honours me.
Thank God, I am not as these rigid fools,
    Even as this Pharisee."

IN MANCHESTER SQUARE

(*In Memoriam* T.H.)

THE paralytic man has dropped in death
   The crossing-sweeper's brush to which he clung,
One-handed, twisted, dwarfed, scanted of breath,
   Although his hair was young.

I saw this year the winter vines of France,
   Dwarfed, twisted goblins in the frosty drouth—
Gnarled, crippled, blackened little stems askance
   On long hills to the South.

Great green and golden hands of leaves ere long
   Shall proffer clusters in that vineyard wide.
And O his might, his sweet, his wine, his song,
   His stature, since he died!

MATERNITY

ONE wept whose only child was dead,
    New-born, ten years ago.
"Weep not ; he is in bliss," they said.
    She answered, "Even so,

"Ten years ago was born in pain
    A child, not now forlorn.
But oh, ten years ago, in vain,
    A mother, a mother was born."

THE FIRST SNOW

NOT yet was winter come to earth's soft floor,
   The tideless wave, the warm white road, the shore,
The serried town whose small street tortuously
      Led darkling to the dazzling sea.

Not yet to breathing man, not to his song,
Not to his comforted heart; not to the long
Close-cultivated lands beneath the hill.
      Summer was gently with them still.

But on the Apennine mustered the cloud;
The grappling storm shut down.   Aloft, aloud,
Ruled secret tempest one long day and night,
      Until another morning's light.

O tender mountain-tops and delicate,
Where summer-long the westering sunlight sate!
Within that fastness darkened from the sun,
      What solitary things were done?

The clouds let go, they rose, they winged away;
Snow-white the altered mountains faced the day,
As saints who keep their counsel sealed and fast,
      Their anguish over-past.

THE COURTS

A FIGURE OF THE EPIPHANY

THE poet's imageries are noble ways,
 Approaches to a plot, an open shrine.
Their splendours, colours, avenues, arrays,
  Their courts that run with wine;

Beautiful similes, "fair and flagrant things,"
Enriched, enamouring,—raptures, metaphors
Enhancing life, are paths for pilgrim kings
  Made free of golden doors.

And yet the open heavenward plot, with dew,
Ultimate poetry, enclosed, enskied,
(Albeit such ceremonies lead thereto)
  Stands on the yonder side.

Plain, behind oracles, it is; and past
All symbols, simple; perfect, heavenly-wild,
The song some loaded poets reach at last—
  The kings that found a Child.

87

THE LAUNCH

FORTH, to the alien gravity,
   Forth, to the laws of ocean, we
  Builders on earth by laws of land
  Entrust this creature of our hand
Upon the calculated sea.

Fast bound to shore we cling, we creep,
And make our ship ready to leap
  Light to the flood, equipped to ride
  The strange conditions of the tide—
New weight, new force, new world : the Deep.

Ah thus—not thus—the Dying, kissed,
Cherished, exhorted, shriven, dismissed ;
  By all the eager means we hold
  We, warm, prepare him for the cold,
To keep the incalculable tryst.

TO THE BODY

THOU inmost, ultimate
   Council of judgment, palace of decrees,
Where the high senses hold their spiritual state,
     Sued by earth's embassies,
And sign, approve, accept, conceive, create;

     Create—thy senses close
With the world's pleas.   The random odours reach
Their sweetness in the place of thy repose,
     Upon thy tongue the peach,
And in thy nostrils breathes the breathing rose.

     To thee, secluded one,
The dark vibrations of the sightless skies,
The lovely inexplicit colours run;
     The light gropes for those eyes.
O thou august! thou dost command the sun.

     Music, all dumb, hath trod
Into thine ear her one effectual way;
And fire and cold approach to gain thy nod,
     Where thou call'st up the day,
Where thou awaitest the appeal of God.

THE UNEXPECTED PERIL

UNLIKE the youth that all men say
    They prize—youth of abounding blood,
In love with the sufficient day,
And gay in growth, and strong in bud;

Unlike was mine! Then my first slumber
    Nightly rehearsed my last; each breath
Knew itself one of the unknown number.
    But Life was urgent with me as Death.

My shroud was in the flocks; the hill
    Within its quarry locked my stone;
My bier grew in the woods; and still
    Life spurred me where I paused alone.

"Begin!" Life called. Again her shout,
    "Make haste while it is called to-day!"
Her exhortations plucked me out,
    Hunted me, turned me, held me at bay.

But if my youth is thus hard pressed
    (I thought) what of a later year?
If the end so threats this tender breast,
    What of the days when it draws near?

Draws near, and little done? yet lo,
    Dread has forborne, and haste lies by.
I was beleaguered; now the foe
    Has raised the siege, I know not why.

THE UNEXPECTED PERIL

I see them troop away; I ask
  Were they in sooth mine enemies—
Terror, the doubt, the lash, the task?
  What heart has my new housemate, Ease?

How am I left, at last, alive,
  To make a stranger of a tear?
What did I do one day to drive
  From me the vigilant angel, Fear?

The diligent angel, Labour? Ay,
  The inexorable angel, Pain?
Menace me, lest indeed I die,
  Sloth! Turn; crush, teach me fear again!

CHRIST IN THE UNIVERSE

WITH this ambiguous earth
    His dealings have been told us.   These abide:
The signal to a maid, the human birth,
The lesson, and the young Man crucified.

    But not a star of all
The innumerable host of stars has heard
How He administered this terrestrial ball.
Our race have kept their Lord's entrusted Word.

    Of His earth-visiting feet
None knows the secret, cherished, perilous,
The terrible, shamefast, frightened, whispered, sweet,
Heart-shattering secret of His way with us.

    No planet knows that this
Our wayside planet, carrying land and wave,
Love and life multiplied, and pain and bliss,
Bears, as chief treasure, one forsaken grave.

    Nor, in our little day,
May His devices with the heavens be guessed,
His pilgrimage to thread the Milky Way,
Or His bestowals there be manifest.

    But, in the eternities,
Doubtless we shall compare together, hear
A million alien Gospels, in what guise
He trod the Pleiades, the Lyre, the Bear.

    O, be prepared, my soul!
To read the inconceivable, to scan
The million forms of God those stars unroll
When, in our turn, we show to them a Man.

BEYOND KNOWLEDGE

" Your sins . . . shall be white as snow."

INTO the rescued world newcomer,
   The newly-dead stepped up, and cried,
"O what is that, sweeter than summer
   Was to my heart before I died?
Sir (to an angel), what is yonder
   More bright than the remembered skies,
A lovelier sight, a softer splendour
   Than when the moon was wont to rise?
Surely no sinner wears such seeming
   Even the Rescued World within?"

"O the success of His redeeming!
   O child, it is a rescued sin!"

93

EASTER NIGHT

ALL night had shout of men and cry
    Of woeful women filled His way;
Until that noon of sombre sky
    On Friday, clamour and display
Smote Him; no solitude had He,
No silence, since Gethsemane.

Public was Death; but Power, but Might,
    But Life again, but Victory,
Were hushed within the dead of night,
    The shutter'd dark, the secrecy.
And all alone, alone, alone
He rose again behind the stone.

A FATHER OF WOMEN

AD SOROREM E. B.

" Thy father was transfused into thy blood."
                    Dryden: Ode to Mrs. Anne Killigrew.

OUR father works in us,
    The daughters of his manhood.   Not undone
Is he, not wasted, though transmuted thus,
        And though he left no son.

            Therefore on him I cry
To arm me : "For my delicate mind a casque,
A breastplate for my heart, courage to die,
        Of thee, captain, I ask.

        "Nor strengthen only ; press
A finger on this violent blood and pale,
Over this rash will let thy tenderness
        A while pause, and prevail.

        "And shepherd-father, thou
Whose staff folded my thoughts before my birth,
Control them now I am of earth, and now
        Thou art no more of earth.

        "O liberal, constant, dear !
Crush in my nature the ungenerous art
Of the inferior ; set me high, and here,
        Here garner up thy heart."

A FATHER OF WOMEN

Like to him now are they,
The million living fathers of the War—
Mourning the crippled world, the bitter day—
Whose striplings are no more.

The crippled world !   Come then,
Fathers of women with your honour in trust ;
Approve, accept, know them daughters of men,
Now that your sons are dust.

LENGTH OF DAYS

TO THE EARLY DEAD IN BATTLE

THERE is no length of days
    But yours, boys who were children once.
  Of old
The Past beset you in your childish ways,
    With sense of Time untold.

    What have you then forgone?
A history? This you had. Or memories?
These, too, you had of your far-distant dawn.
    No further dawn seems his,

    The old man who shares with you,
But has no more, no more. Time's mystery
Did once for him the most that it can do;
    He has had infancy.

    And all his dreams, and all
His loves for mighty Nature, sweet and few,
Are but the dwindling past he can recall
    Of what his childhood knew.

    He counts not any more
His brief, his present years. But O he knows
How far apart the summers were of yore,
    How far apart the snows.

    Therefore be satisfied;
Long life is in your treasury ere you fall;
Yes, and first love, like Dante's. O a bride
    For ever mystical!

LENGTH OF DAYS

Irrevocable good,—
You dead, and now about, so young, to die,—
Your childhood was; there Space, there Multi-
    tude,
There dwelt Antiquity.

NURSE EDITH CAVELL

Two o'clock, the morning of October 12th, 1915

TO her accustomed eyes
   The midnight-morning brought not such a dread
As thrills the chance-awakened head that lies
In trivial sleep on the habitual bed.

     'Twas yet some hours ere light;
And many, many, many a break of day
Had she outwatched the dying; but this night
Shortened her vigil was, briefer the way.

     By dial of the clock
'Twas day in the dark above her lonely head.
"This day thou shalt be with Me." Ere the cock
Announced that day she met the Immortal Dead.

SUMMER IN ENGLAND, 1914

ON London fell a clearer light;
 Caressing pencils of the sun
Defined the distances, the white
 Houses transfigured one by one,
The "long, unlovely street" impearled.
O what a sky has walked the world!

Most happy year! And out of town
 The hay was prosperous, and the wheat;
The silken harvest climbed the down:
 Moon after moon was heavenly-sweet
Stroking the bread within the sheaves,
Looking 'twixt apples and their leaves.

And while this rose made round her cup,
 The armies died convulsed. And when
This chaste young silver sun went up
 Softly, a thousand shattered men,
One wet corruption, heaped the plain,
After a league-long throb of pain.

Flower following tender flower; and birds,
 And berries; and benignant skies
Made thrive the serried flocks and herds.—
 Yonder are men shot through the eyes.
  Love, hide thy face
From man's unpardonable race.

  * * *

Who said "No man hath greater love than this,
 To die to serve his friend"?
So these have loved us all unto the end.
 Chide thou no more, O thou unsacrificed!
The soldier dying dies upon a kiss,
 The very kiss of Christ.

TO TINTORETTO IN VENICE

*The Art of Painting had in the Primitive years looked
with the light, not towards it. Before Tintoretto's date,
however, many painters practised shadows and lights, and
turned more or less sunwards; but he set the figure between
himself and a full sun. His work is to be known in Venice
by the splendid trick of an occluded sun and a shadow thrown
straight at the spectator.*

MASTER, thy enterprise,
    Magnificent, magnanimous, was well done,
Which seized the head of Art, and turned her eyes—
The simpleton—and made her front the sun.

    Long had she sat content,
Her young unlessoned back to a morning gay,
To a solemn noon, to a cloudy firmament,
And looked upon a world in gentle day.

    But thy imperial call
Bade her to stand with thee and breast the light,
And therefore face the shadows, mystical,
Sombre, translucent, vestiges of night,

    Yet glories of the day.
Eagle! we know thee by thy undaunted eyes
Sky-ward, and by thy glooms; we know thy way
Ambiguous, and those halo-misted dyes.

    Thou Cloud, the bridegroom's friend
(The bridegroom sun)! Master, we know thy sign:
A mystery of hues world-without-end;
And hide-and-seek of gamesome and divine;

101

TO TINTORETTO IN VENICE

Shade of the noble head
Cast hitherward upon the noble breast;
Human solemnities thrice hallowèd;
The haste to Calvary, the Cross at rest.

Look sunward, Angel, then!
Carry the fortress-heavens by that hand;
Still be the interpreter of suns to men;
And shadow us, O thou Tower! for thou shalt stand.

A THRUSH BEFORE DAWN

A VOICE peals in this end of night
    A phrase of notes resembling stars,
Single and spiritual notes of light.
    What call they at my window-bars?
        The South, the past, the day to be,
        An ancient infelicity.

Darkling, deliberate, what sings
    This wonderful one, alone, at peace?
What wilder things than song, what things
    Sweeter than youth, clearer than Greece,
        Dearer than Italy, untold
        Delight, and freshness centuries old?

And first first-loves, a multitude,
    The exaltation of their pain;
Ancestral childhood long renewed;
    And midnights of invisible rain;
        And gardens, gardens, night and day,
        Gardens and childhood all the way.

What Middle Ages passionate,
    O passionless voice! What distant bells
Lodged in the hills, what palace state
    Illyrian! For it speaks, it tells,
        Without desire, without dismay,
        Some morrow and some yesterday.

All-natural things! But more—Whence came
    This yet remoter mystery?
How do these starry notes proclaim
    A graver still divinity?
        This hope, this sanctity of fear?
        O innocent throat! O human ear!

THE TWO SHAKESPEARE
TERCENTENARIES

OF BIRTH, 1864; OF DEATH, 1916

TO SHAKESPEARE

LONGER than thine, than thine,
    Is now my time of life; and thus thy years
Seem to be clasped and harboured within mine.
O how ignoble this my clasp appears!

      Thy unprophetic birth,
Thy darkling death: living I might have seen
That cradle, marked those labours, closed that earth.
O first, O last, O infinite between!

      Now that my life has shared
Thy dedicated date, O mortal, twice,
To what all-vain embrace shall be compared
My lean enclosure of thy paradise:

      To ignorant arms that fold
A poet to a foolish breast? The Line,
That is not, with the world within its hold?
So, days with days, my days encompass thine.

      Child, Stripling, Man—the sod.
Might I talk little language to thee, pore
On thy last silence? O thou city of God,
My waste lies after thee, and lies before.

TO O——, OF HER DARK EYES

ACROSS what calm of tropic seas,
    'Neath alien clusters of the nights,
Looked, in the past, such eyes as these !
    Long-quenched, relumed, ancestral lights !

The generations fostered them ;
    And steadfast Nature, secretwise—
Thou seedling child of that old stem—
    Kindled anew thy dark-bright eyes.

Was it a century or two
    This lovely darkness rose and set,
Occluded by grey eyes and blue,
    And Nature feigning to forget?

Some grandam gave a hint of it—
    So cherished was it in thy race,
So fine a treasure to transmit
    In its perfection to thy face.

Some father to some mother's breast
    Entrusted it, unknowing. Time
Implied, or made it manifest,
    Bequest of a forgotten clime.

Hereditary eyes ! But this
    Is single, singular, apart :—
New-made thy love, new-made thy kiss,
    New-made thy errand to my heart.

THE TREASURE

THREE times have I beheld
   Fear leap in a babe's face, and take his breath,
     Fear, like the fear of eld
That knows the price of life, the name of death.

     What is it justifies
This thing, this dread, this fright that has no tongue,
     The terror in those eyes
When only eyes can speak—they are so young?

     Not yet those eyes had wept.
What does fear cherish that it locks so well?
     What fortress is thus kept?
Of what is ignorant terror sentinel?

     And pain in the poor child,
Monstrously disproportionate, and dumb
     In the poor beast, and wild
In the old decorous man, caught, overcome?

     Of what the outposts these?
Of what the fighting guardians? What demands
     That sense of menaces,
And then such flying feet, imploring hands?

     Life: There's nought else to seek;
Life only, little prized; but by design
     Of nature prized. How weak,
How sad, how brief! O how divine, divine!

A WIND OF CLEAR WEATHER
IN ENGLAND

O WHAT a miracle wind is this
  Has crossed the English land to-day
With an unprecedented kiss,
  And wonderfully found a way!

Unsmirched incredibly and clean,
  Between the towns and factories,
Avoiding, has his long flight been,
  Bringing a sky like Sicily's.

O fine escape, horizon pure
  As Rome's!   Black chimneys left and right,
But not for him, the straight, the sure,
  His luminous day, his spacious night.

How keen his choice, how swift his feet!
  Narrow the way and hard to find!
This delicate stepper and discreet
  Walked not like any worldly wind.

Most like a man in man's own day,
  One of the few, a perfect one:
His open earth—the single way;
  His narrow road—the open sun.

IN SLEEP

I DREAMT (no "dream" awake—a dream indeed)
A wrathful man was talking in the park :
"Where are the Higher Powers, who know our need
And leave us in the dark?

"There are no Higher Powers ; there is no heart
In God, no love"—his oratory here,
Taking the paupers' and the cripples' part,
Was broken by a tear.

And then it seemed that One who did create
Compassion, who alone invented pity,
Walked, as though called, in at that north-east gate,
Out from the muttering city ;

Threaded the little crowd, trod the brown grass,
Bent o'er the speaker close, saw the tear rise,
And saw Himself, as one looks in a glass,
In those impassioned eyes.

THE DIVINE PRIVILEGE

LORD, where are Thy prerogatives?
     Why, men have more than Thou hast kept;
The king rewards, remits, forgives,
     The poet to a throne has stept.

And Thou, despoiled, hast given away
     Worship to men, success to strife,
Thy glory to the heavenly day,
     And made Thy sun the lord of life.

Is one too precious to impart,
     One property reserved to Christ,
One, cherished, grappled to that heart?
     —To be alone the Sacrificed?

O Thou who lovest to redeem!—
     One whom I know lies sore oppressed.
Thou wilt not suffer me to dream
     That I can bargain for her rest.

Seven hours I swiftly sleep, while she
     Measures the leagues of dark, awake.
O that my dewy eyes might be
     Parched by a vigil for her sake!

But O rejected! O in vain!
     I cannot give who would not keep.
I cannot buy, I cannot gain,
     I cannot give her half my sleep.

FREE WILL

DEAR are some hidden things
 My soul has sealed in silence; past delights;
Hope unconfessed; desires with hampered wings,
 Remembered in the nights.

But my best treasures are
 Ignoble, undelightful, abject, cold;
Yet O! profounder hoards oracular
 No reliquaries hold.

There lie my trespasses,
 Abjured but not disowned. I'll not accuse
Determinism, nor, as the Master* says,
 Charge even "the poor Deuce."

Under my hand they lie,
 My very own, my proved iniquities;
And though the glory of my life go by
 I hold and garner these.

How else, how otherwhere,
 How otherwise, shall I discern and grope
For lowliness? How hate, how love, how dare,
 How weep, how hope?

* George Meredith.

THE TWO QUESTIONS

" A RIDDLING world!" one cried.
     "If pangs must be, would God that they were sent
To the impure, the cruel, and passed aside
     The holy innocent!"

     But I, "Ah no, no, no!
Not the clean heart transpierced; not tears that fall
For a child's agony; nor a martyr's woe;
     Not these, not these appal.

     "Not docile motherhood,
Dutiful, frequent, closed in all distress;
Not shedding of the unoffending blood;
     Not little joy grown less;

     "Not all-benign old age
With dotage mocked; not gallantry that faints
And still pursues; not the vile heritage
     Of sin's disease in saints;

     "Not these defeat the mind.
For great is that abjection, and august
That irony. Submissive we shall find
     A splendour in that dust.

     "Not these puzzle the will;
Not these the yet unanswered question urge.
But the unjust stricken; but the hands that kill
     Lopped; but the merited scourge;

     "The sensualist at fast;
The merciless felled; the liar in his snares.
The cowardice of my judgment sees, aghast,
     The flail, the chaff, the tares."

THE LORD'S PRAYER

"Audemus dicere 'Pater Noster.'"—CANON OF
THE MASS.

THERE is a bolder way,
  There is a wilder enterprise than this
All-human iteration day by day.
Courage, mankind ! Restore Him what is His.

      Out of His mouth were given
These phrases. O replace them whence they came.
He, only, knows our inconceivable "Heaven,"
Our hidden "Father," and the unspoken "Name";

      Our "trespasses," our "bread,"
The "will" inexorable yet implored ;
The miracle-words that are and are not said,
Charged with the unknown purpose of their Lord.

      "Forgive," "give," "lead us not"—
Speak them by Him, O man the unaware,
Speak by that dear tongue, though thou know not what,
Shuddering through the paradox of prayer.

Last Poems

THE POET AND HIS BOOK

HERE are my thoughts, alive within this fold,
  My simple sheep.   Their shepherd, I grow wise
As dearly, gravely, deeply I behold
      Their different eyes.

O distant pastures in their blood ! O streams
  From watersheds that fed them for this prison !
Lights from aloft, midsummer suns in dreams,
      Set and arisen.

They wander out, but all return anew,
  The small ones, to this heart to which they clung;
"And those that are with young," the fruitful few
      That are with young.

INTIMATIONS OF MORTALITY

FROM RECOLLECTIONS OF EARLY CHILDHOOD

> A simple child . . .
>   That lightly draws its breath
> And feels its life in every limb,
>   What should it know of death?
>   WORDSWORTH.

IT knows but will not tell.
   Awake, alone, it counts its father's years—
How few are left—its mother's.   Ah, how well
   It knows of death, in tears.

If any of the three—
   Parents and child—believe they have prevailed
To keep the secret of mortality,
   I know that two have failed.

The third, the lonely, keeps
   One secret—a child's knowledge. When they come
At night to ask wherefore the sweet one weeps,
   Those hidden lips are dumb.

THE WIND IS BLIND

"EYELESS, IN GAZA, AT THE MILL, WITH SLAVES"
Milton's "Samson."

THE wind is blind.
    The earth sees sun and moon; the height
Is watch-tower to the dawn; the plain
Shines to the summer; visible light
    Is scattered in the drops of rain.

        The wind is blind.
The flashing billows are aware;
    With open eyes the cities see;
Light leaves the ether, everywhere
    Known to the homing bird and bee.

        The wind is blind,
Is blind alone.   How has he hurled
    His ignorant lash, his aimless dart,
His eyeless rush upon the world,
    Unseeing, to break his unknown heart!

        The wind is blind,
And the sail traps him, and the mill
    Captures him; and he cannot save
His swiftness and his desperate will
    From those blind uses of the slave.

TIME'S REVERSALS

A DAUGHTER'S PARADOX

To his devoted heart *
    Who, young, had loved his ageing mate for life,
In late lone years Time gave the elder's part,
    Time gave the bridegroom's boast, Time gave a younger
      wife.

A wilder prank and plot
    Time soon will promise, threaten, offering me
Impossible things that Nature suffers not—
    A daughter's riper mind, a child's seniority.

Oh, by my filial tears
    Mourned all too young, Father ! On this my head
Time yet will force at last the longer years,
    Claiming some strange respect for me from you, the dead.

Nay, nay ! Too new to know
    Time's conjuring is, too great to understand.
Memory has not died ; it leaves me so—
    Leaning a fading brow on your unfaded hand.

   * *Samuel Johnson outlived by thirty years his wife, who was twenty years his senior.*

THE THRESHING MACHINE

NO "fan is in his hand" for these
    Young villagers beneath the trees,
Watching the wheels. But I recall
The rhythm of rods that rise and fall,
Purging the harvest, over-seas.

No fan, no flail, no threshing-floor !
And all their symbols evermore
    Forgone in England now—the sign,
    The visible pledge, the threat divine,
The chaff dispersed, the wheat in store.

The unbreathing engine marks no tune,
Steady at sunrise, steady at noon,
    Inhuman, perfect, saving time,
    And saving measure, and saving rhyme—
And did our Ruskin speak too soon?

"No noble strength on earth" he sees
"Save Hercules' arm" ; his grave decrees
    Curse wheel and steam. As the wheels ran
    I saw the other strength of man,
I knew the brain of Hercules.

WINTER TREES ON THE HORIZON

O DELICATE ! Even in wooded lands
　　They show the margin of my world,
My own horizon ; little bands
　　Of twigs unveil that edge impearled.

And what is more mine own than this,
　　My limit, level with mine eyes?
For me precisely do they kiss—
　　The rounded earth, the rounding skies.

It has my stature, that keen line
　　(Let mathematics vouch for it).
The lark's horizon is not mine,
　　No, nor his nestlings' where they sit ;

No, nor the child's. And, when I gain
　　The hills, I lift it as I rise
Erect ; anon, back to the plain
　　I soothe it with mine equal eyes.

TO SLEEP

DEAR fool, be true to me!
    I know the poets speak thee fair, and I
      Hail thee uncivilly.
O but I call with a more urgent cry!

      I do not prize thee less,
I need thee more, that thou dost love to teach—
      Father of foolishness—
The imbecile dreams clear out of wisdom's reach.

      Come and release me; bring
My irresponsible mind; come in thy hours.
      Draw from my soul the sting
Of wit that trembles, consciousness that cowers.

      For if night comes without thee
She is more cruel than day. But thou, fulfil
      Thy work, thy gifts about thee—
Liberty, liberty, from this weight of will.

      My day-mind can endure
Upright, in hope, all it must undergo.
      But O afraid, unsure,
My night-mind waking lies too low, too low.

      Dear fool, be true to me!
The night is thine, man yields it, it beseems
      Thy ironic dignity.
Make me all night the innocent fool that dreams.

"THE MARRIAGE OF TRUE MINDS"

(IN THE BACH-GOUNOD "AVE MARIA")

THAT seeking Prelude found its unforetold
    Unguessed intention, trend;
Though needing no fulfilment, did enfold
    This exquisite end.

Bach led his notes up through their delicate slope
    Aspiring, so they sound,
And so they were—in some strange ignorant hope
    Thus to be crowned.

What deep soft seas beneath this buoyant barque!
    What winds to speed this bird!
What impulses to toss this heavenward lark!
    Thought—then the word.

Lovely the tune, lovely the unconsciousness
    Of him who promised it.
Lovely the years that joined in blessedness
    The two, the fit.

Bach was Precursor. But no Baptist's cry
    Was his; he, who began
For one who was to end, did prophesy,
    By Nature's generous act, the lesser man.

IN HONOUR OF AMERICA, 1917

IN ANTITHESIS TO ROSSETTI'S "ON THE REFUSAL
OF AID BETWEEN NATIONS"

NOT that the earth is changing, O my God!
　　Not that her brave democracies take heart
　To share, to rule her treasure, to impart
The wine to those who long the wine-press trod;
Not therefore trust we that beneath Thy nod,
　Thy silent benediction, even now
　In gratitude so many nations bow,
So many poor: not therefore, O my God!

But because living men for dying man
　Go to a million deaths, to deal one blow;
　And justice speaks one great compassionate tongue;
And nation unto nation calls "One clan
　We succourers are, one tribe!" By this we know
Our earth holds confident, steadfast, being young.

"LORD, I OWE THEE A DEATH"

Richard Hooker

(IN TIME OF WAR)

MAN pays that debt with new munificence,
    Not piecemeal now, not slowly, by the old:
Not grudgingly, by the effaced thin pence,
    But greatly and in gold.

REFLEXIONS

(I) IN IRELAND

A MIRROR faced a mirror : ire and hate
    Opposite ire and hate ; the multiplied,
The complex charge rejected, intricate,
    From side to sullen side ;

One plot, one crime, one treachery, nay, one name,
    Assumed, denounced, in echoes of replies.
The doubt, exchanged, lit thousands of one flame
    Within those mutual eyes.

(II) IN "OTHELLO"

A MIRROR faced a mirror : in sweet pain
    His dangers with her pity did she track,
Received her pity with his love again,
    And these she wafted back.

That masculine passion in her little breast
    She bandied with him ; her compassion he
Bandied with her. What tender sport ! No rest
    Had love's infinity.

REFLEXIONS

(III) IN TWO POETS

A MIRROR faced a mirror : O thy word,
   Thou lord of images, did lodge in me,
Locked to my heart, homing from home, a bird,
   A carrier, bound for thee.

Thy migratory greatness, greater far
   For that return, returns ; now grow divine
By endlessness my visiting thoughts, that are
   Those visiting thoughts of thine.

TO CONSCRIPTS

"Compel them to come in."—ST. LUKE'S GOSPEL

YOU "made a virtue of necessity"
   By divine sanction ; you, the loth, the grey,
The random, gentle, unconvinced ; O be
   The crowned !—you may, you may.

You, the compelled, be feasted !   You, the caught,
   Be freemen of the gates that word unlocks !
Accept your victory from that unsought,
   That heavenly paradox.

THE VOICE OF A BIRD

"He shall rise up at the voice of a bird."—

ECCLESIASTES

WHO then is "he"?
  Dante, Keats, Shakespeare, Milton, Shelley; all
Rose in their greatness at the shrill decree,
  The little rousing inarticulate call.

  For they stood up
At the bird-voice, of lark, of nightingale,
Drank poems from that throat as from a cup.
Over the great world's notes did these prevail.

  And not alone
The signal poets woke. In listening man,
Woman, and child a poet stirs unknown,
Throughout the Mays of birds since Mays began.

  He rose, he heard—
Our father, our St. Peter, in his tears—
The crowing, twice, of the prophetic bird,
The saddest cock-crow of our human years.

THE QUESTION

IL POETA MI DISSE, "CHE PENSI?"

VIRGIL stayed Dante with a wayside word;
  But long, and low, and loud and urgently
The poets of my passion have I heard
    Summoning me.

It is their closest whisper and their call.
Their greatness to this lowliness hath spoken,
Their voices rest upon that interval,
    Their sign, their token.

Man at his little prayer tells Heaven his thought,
To man entrusts his thought—"Friend, this is mine."
The immortal poets within my breast have sought,
    Saying, "What is thine?"

THE LAWS OF VERSE

DEAR laws, come to my breast!
    Take all my frame, and make your close arms meet
Around me; and so ruled, so warmed, so pressed,
I breathe, aware; I feel my wild heart beat.

        Dear laws, be wings to me!
The feather merely floats. O be it heard
Through weight of life—the skylark's gravity—
That I am not a feather, but a bird.

"THE RETURN TO NATURE"

Histories of Modern Poetry

(I) PROMETHEUS

IT was the south : mid-everything,
    Mid-land, midsummer, noon ;
And deep within a limpid spring
    The mirrored sun of June.

Splendour in freshness ! Ah, who stole
    This sun, this fire, from heaven?
He holds it shining in his soul,
    Prometheus the forgiven.

(II) THETIS

In her bright title poets dare
    What the wild eye of fancy sees—
Similitude—the clear, the fair
    Light mystery of images.

Round the blue sea I love the best
    The argent foam played, slender, fleet ;
I saw—past Wordsworth and the rest—
    Her natural, Greek, and silver feet.

TO SILENCE

"SPACE, THE BOUND OF A SOLID": SILENCE, THEN,
THE FORM OF A MELODY

NOT, Silence, for thine idleness I raise
    My silence-bounded singing in thy praise,
But for thy moulding of my Mozart's tune,
Thy hold upon the bird that sings the moon,
    Thy magisterial ways.

Man's lovely definite melody-shapes are thine,
Outlined, controlled, compressed, complete, divine.
Also thy fine intrusions do I trace,
Thy afterthoughts, thy wandering, thy grace,
    Within the poet's line.

Thy secret is the song that is to be.
Music had never stature but for thee,
Sculptor ! strong as the sculptor Space whose hand
Urged the Discobolus and bade him stand.

    *   *   *   *   *

Man, on his way to Silence, stops to hear and see.

THE ENGLISH METRES

THE rooted liberty of flowers in breeze
    Is theirs, by national luck impulsive, terse,
Tethered, uncaptured, rules obeyed "at ease,"
    Time-strengthened laws of verse.

Or they are like our seasons that admit
    Inflexion, not infraction : Autumn hoar,
Winter more tender than our thoughts of it,
    But a year's steadfast four ;

Redundant syllables of Summer rain,
    And displaced accents of authentic Spring ;
Spondaic clouds above a gusty plain
    With dactyls on the wing.

Not Common Law, but Equity, is theirs—
    Our metres ; play and agile foot askance,
And distant, beckoning, blithely rhyming pairs,
    Unknown to classic France ;

Unknown to Italy.   Ay, count, collate,
    Latins ! with eye foreseeing on the time,
And numbered fingers, and approaching fate
    On the appropriate rhyme.

Nay, nobly our grave measures are decreed :
    Heroic, Alexandrine with the stay,
Deliberate ; or else like him whose speed
    Did outrun Peter, urgent in the break of day.

"RIVERS UNKNOWN TO SONG"

James Thomson

WIDE waters in the waste; or, out of reach,
   Rough Alpine falls where late a glacier hung;
Or rivers groping for the alien beach,
   Through continents, unsung.

Nay, not these nameless, these remote, alone;
   But all the streams from all the watersheds—
Peneus, Danube, Nile—are the unknown
   Young in their ancient beds.

Man has no tale for them. O travellers swift
   From secrets to oblivion! Waters wild
That pass in act to bend a flower, or lift
   The bright limbs of a child!

For they are new, they are fresh; there's no surprise
   Like theirs on earth. O strange for evermore!
This moment's Tiber with his shining eyes
   Never saw Rome before.

Man has no word for their eternity—
   Rhine, Avon, Arno, younglings, youth uncrowned:
Ignorant, innocent, instantaneous, free,
   Unwelcomed, unrenowned.

TO THE MOTHER OF CHRIST
THE SON OF MAN

WE too (one cried), we too,
    We the unready, the perplexed, the cold,
Must shape the Eternal in our thoughts anew,
    Cherish, possess, enfold.

    Thou sweetly, we in strife.
It is our passion to conceive Him thus
In mind, in sense, within our house of life ;
    That seed is locked in us.

    We must affirm our Son
From the ambiguous Nature's difficult speech,
Gather in darkness that resplendent One,
    Close as our grasp can reach.

    Nor shall we ever rest
From this our task. An hour sufficed for thee,
Thou innocent ! He lingers in the breast
    Of our humanity.

A COMPARISON IN A SEASIDE FIELD

'TIS royal and authentic June
 Over this poor soil blossoming;
Here lies, beneath an upright noon,
 Thin nation for so wild a king.

Far off, the noble Summer rules,
 Violent in the ardent rose,
His sun alight in mirroring pools,
 Braggart on Alps of vanquished snows;

Away, aloft, true to his hour,
 Announced, his colour, his fire, his jest.
But here, in negligible flower,
 Summer is not proclaimed :—confessed.

A woman I marked; for her no state,
 Small joy, no song. She had her boon,
Her only youth, true to its date,
 Faintly perceptible, her June.

SURMISE

NOT wish, nor fear, nor quite expectancy
   Is that vague spirit Surmise,
That wanderer, that wonderer, whom we see
   Within each other's eyes;

And yet not often. For she flits away,
   Fitful as infant thought,
Visitant at a venture, hope at play,
   Unversed in facts, untaught.

In "the wide fields of possibility"
   Surmise, conjecturing,
Makes little trials, incredulous, that flee
   Abroad on random wing.

One day this inarticulate shall find speech,
   This hoverer seize our breath.
Surmise shall close with man—with all, with each—
In her own sovereign hour, the moments of our death.

TO ANTIQUITY

"... REVERENCE FOR OUR FATHERS, WITH THEIR
STORES OF EXPERIENCES"
An author whose name I did not note

O OUR young ancestor,
　　Our boy in Letters, how we trudge oppressed
With our "experiences," and you of yore
　　Flew light, and blessed !

Youngling, in your new town,
　　Tight, like a box of toys—the town that is
Our shattered, open ruin, with its crown
　　Of histories ;

You with your morning words,
　　Fresh from the night, your yet un-sonneted moon,
Your passion undismayed, cool as a bird's
　　Ignorant tune ;

O youngling ! how is this ?
　　Your poems are not wearied yet, not dead,
Must I bow low ? or, with an envious kiss,
　　Put you to bed ?

CHRISTMAS NIGHT

"IF I CANNOT SEE THEE PRESENT I WILL MOURN
THEE ABSENT, FOR THIS ALSO IS A PROOF OF LOVE"
Thomas à Kempis

WE do not find Him on the difficult earth,
  In surging human-kind,
In wayside death or accidental birth,
  Or in the "march of mind."

Nature, her nests, her prey, the fed, the caught,
  Hide Him so well, so well,
His steadfast secret there seems to our thought
  Life's saddest miracle.

He's but conjectured in man's happiness,
  Suspected in man's tears,
Or lurks beyond the long, discouraged guess,
  Grown fainter through the years.

    *   *   *   *   *

But absent, absent now? Ah, what is this,
  Near as in child-birth bed,
Laid on our sorrowful hearts, close to a kiss?
  A homeless childish head.

139

THE OCTOBER REDBREAST

AUTUMN is weary, halt, and old;
    Ah, but she owns the song of joy!
Her colours fade, her woods are cold.
    Her singing-bird's a boy, a boy.

In lovely Spring the birds were bent
    On nests, on use, on love, forsooth!
Grown-up were they. This boy's content,
    For his is liberty, his is youth.

The musical stripling sings for play
    Taking no thought, and virgin-glad.
For duty sang those mates in May.
    This singing-bird's a lad, a lad.

TO "A CERTAIN RICH MAN"

"I HAVE FIVE BRETHREN. . . . FATHER, I BESEECH
THEE . . . LEST THEY COME TO THIS PLACE"

St. Luke's Gospel

THOU wouldst not part thy spoil
    Gained from the beggar's want, the weakling's toil,
Nor spare a jot of sumptuousness or state
For Lazarus at the gate.

And in the appalling night
Of expiation, as in day's delight,
Thou heldst thy niggard hand; it would not share
One hour of thy despair.

Those five—thy prayer for them!
O generous! who, condemned, wouldst not condemn,
Whose ultimate human greatness proved thee so
A miser of thy woe.

"EVERLASTING FAREWELLS ! AND AGAIN, AND
YET AGAIN . . . EVERLASTING FAREWELLS !"

De Quincey

"FAREWELLS!"   O what a word !
  Denying this agony, denying the affrights,
Denying all De Quincey spoke or heard
In the infernal sadness of his nights.

  How mean these strange "farewells"?
"Vale"? "Addio"? "Leb'wohl"? Not one but seems
A tranquil refutation; tolling bells
That yet behold the terror of his dreams.

THE POET TO THE BIRDS

YOU bid me hold my peace,
  Or so I think, you birds; you'll not forgive
My kill-joy song that makes the wild song cease,
  Silent or fugitive.

Yon thrush stopt in mid-phrase
  At my mere footfall; and a longer note
Took wing and fled afield, and went its ways
  Within the blackbird's throat.

Hereditary song,
  Illyrian lark and Paduan nightingale,
Is yours, unchangeable the ages long;
  Assyria heard your tale;

Therefore you do not die.
  But single, local, lonely, mortal, new,
Unlike, and thus like all my race, am I,
  Preluding my adieu.

My human song must be
  My human thought. Be patient till 'tis done.
I shall not hold my little peace; for me
  There is no peace but one.

AT NIGHT

To W. M.

HOME, home from the horizon far and clear,
    Hither the soft wings sweep;
Flocks of the memories of the day draw near
    The dovecote doors of sleep.

Oh, which are they that come through sweetest light
    Of all these homing birds?
Which with the straightest and the swiftest flight?
    Your words to me, your words!